SEIZE THE MOMENT

A story of

COURAGE & CHOICE.

By Paula Tatters

ISBN: 978-1-9101-0287-9 (P/B)
ISBN: 978-1-3999-3557-9 (eBook)
ISBN: 978-1-3999-3563-0 (POD)

Book Cover Art:
Robert Crombie
Paula Tatters

Published by:
Angela Curtis
Kin & Kingdoms Books
Tauranga
New Zealand
www.kinandkingdomsbooks.com

I Dedicate this Book to

my wonderful husband Graham
and our two amazing sons,
Stuart and Graham.

Contents

Preface

There I was, in the Pro Shop (golf equipment shop), telling the professional about my poor memory and how I was going to have to give up golf because it was so bad. He said to me, “Paula, what you do is, you tell everybody that you have a bad memory, and they will help you count, and that way you will be able to continue with the golf”.

Three years ago, my memory was so bad that I thought I was on the way to developing dementia. I had been taking care of my mother-in-law for two years at home and in hospital and I knew the symptoms. I couldn’t cook, I couldn’t co-ordinate, I couldn’t take care of my grandchildren without worrying about what I was going to do and about what I was going to forget.

Making appointments was a nightmare; I had to phone people the night before and ask them to phone me in the morning. I also had stickers all over the kitchen to make sure that I wouldn’t forget anything. When I was speaking to people, I was afraid that once I had started the sentence, I wouldn’t get to the end of it, so I was always nervous when speaking.

Then gradually I lost confidence; I didn’t want to go into places in case I would forget what I was going in there for.

One day I went to visit my friend Kate for coffee and on the way out her husband asked if she had told me about the new products she was using. I didn’t know what products he was talking about, so he showed me his hand.

“I had an injury on the palm of my hand,” he said. “It was weeping, and I couldn’t get it to heal, so a friend of mine told me about a product that would help”. He showed me his hand, and it hardly had a mark on it. Then he showed me on a video how bad it had been previously, and how it had really healed up. There was only a very small scar left now.

Kate then told me about a product that was supposed to help memory. She said that it was not yet available in the UK but that it would be soon. I asked her to let me know when it became available. Two months later I was able to order it and I've never looked back.

From the very first day of taking it, my memory started to improve. It was amazing; within a month my memory was good, within two months it was fantastic, within three months it was 3-D, that means I know where I put it, when I put it, and how it is sitting. Unbelievable!

I have been on these products now for three years and my brain now has great clarity, so much so that I was so excited I just wanted to write a book. I have had the most amazing life, and it tickles me pink because I can remember it enough to share it with you through these pages.

My Youth

I was born in Southern Ireland on the 27th of September in 1947. I was the fifth child of nine births. Before I was born, my parents had lost twins and a son. They owned two shops in Limerick and life was pretty good.

However, my dad started on the demon drink and the socialising that went along with drinking sessions. This created problems and they had to sell one shop, as my mum was finding it difficult to cope. Eventually, they split up and my dad moved to London to work.

Being from a catholic family, they sent me to a convent school in Ireland. It was a disaster from day one. All lessons were in Irish, and I could only speak English. Maybe it was me, but the nuns were not a great help. The more they shouted, the less I learned and the more I cried.

Because my parents were having a difficult time together, our family split up. My dad had moved to London and found work, and whilst he was away, my mum had started an affair with an Irish police officer. When he left the police force, my mum and he decided to move to Liverpool.

My two brothers, Desmond and Brian, were left in Ireland; myself and my three sisters, Deidra, Hilda and Marion, moved to England to be near to the family of my mum's new man. It was when I first attended school in Liverpool at ten years of age, that I discovered I was completely illiterate. I was assessed and put into the special class to see if that would help. However, I only stayed in Liverpool for six months, but I picked up some basic literacy skills.

The move to Liverpool was harrowing, so in an effort to make the situation easier to accept, we were told that my dad had died! However, unbeknown to me, my dad was searching for us.

He was aware that my mum's new man had family living in Liverpool, and knew we would attend Sunday Mass, so he started his search there. It was a smart thing to do, as I went to church every Sunday.

One day at Mass, I heard a man coughing in the church which sounded exactly like my dad. At the end of the service, I left the church, and he was outside waiting for me. He was not dead, and he had found his family.

Following that surprise, we met occasionally, and I remember he bought me the most beautiful coat. In an effort to rekindle the relationship, I arranged for my parents to meet at the Adelphi Hotel in Liverpool. They talked and talked for what seemed to me like an age, and eventually they agreed to get back together.

They decided to move to London, where they planned to buy a house. To allow my parents to make a fresh start in London, I was shipped back to my granny's house in Ireland, along with my three sisters.

So, there I was, at eleven years of age, put on a ferry and shipped back across the Irish sea. There we were, three children, two suitcases and one bag.

"Three children, two suitcases, one bag," I kept repeating.

"3, 2, 1, 3, 2, 1, 3, 2, 1."

The boat crossing was so horrendous, the sea was rough, all the seats were occupied, so we had to sit in the corridor where people were being seasick. It was a terrible experience for everyone on board, let alone four frightened, unaccompanied children. We huddled together, and I forgot the golden rule about not talking to strangers.

"Can you help me?" I eventually asked one of the stewards. "I'm on my own with the children."

He went to see the captain, and they allowed us to disembark first, and he delegated someone to help us onto the train. When we got on the train, he felt sorry for us and gave us some food and something to drink, something I remember vividly to this day. Thank God for that guard.

Eventually, after the terrible journey, we got into Limerick City to what I thought was the safety of our aunt and granny. Little did I know we had just been transferred from the frying pan to the fire. One of my sisters, who had been so traumatised by the whole experience of the journey, wet herself in my aunt's car. That night, as a punishment, she was locked in the outside toilet.

It was at this point I just lost it. I jumped onto my aunt's back and started fighting and screaming at her to bring my sister back into the house. Eventually, my aunt relented and allowed her in. But by that time, my sister was in bits. Not a great first night; unfortunately, it did not get any better.

The next few months were not the best of my life, so I was beyond relieved when my parents got settled and sent for us to join them in London.

We moved to London where Mum and Dad had purchased a house in Lewisham. At the age of twelve, I started another convent school. But at least this time I was being taught in English. I was offered some help with my reading and writing; the nuns were very pleasant and for the first time in my life, I discovered sport.

I loved netball, running and gymnastics. I had a brilliant teacher, Miss Patel, who took me under her wing and took me to netball training for Kent County. Driving through busy London in her tiny bubble car amidst the noisy traffic was quite a formidable experience.

Miss Patel was not a nun, but later in life, she took her vows and entered a silent convent. For several years we kept in contact and I still to this day appreciate the positive influence she had on my career and life.

I left school at the age of fourteen years and nine months, so I really only had two years and nine months schooling. I had learned to read and write at that time, and my one and only qualification on leaving school was an RSA certificate for typing at

30 words per minute.

Home life was not terrific; the relationship between Mum and Dad revolved around drinking and fighting with a Mass every Sunday. None of which I wanted to be part of.

So, the first thing I did after leaving school was to move out of 88 Mount Pleasant and into a flat in Ladywell, Southeast London. It had one bedroom, a shared bathroom, and a small area for cooking and washing up. The great thing was, it was very near to a bus stop, so I could travel where I wanted.

It was also next to the swimming pool where I swam most evenings. I attended classes for lifesaving and at 16 years old I qualified as a lifesaving instructor. To help ends meet, I got a Saturday job in a hair salon which was just around the corner. It was an extremely busy salon; Enrico from Italy was fully booked all day.

I shampooed hair, swept the floor, and made tea and coffee for everyone. I smiled a lot and enjoyed my Saturday job. Little did I know how useful that experience would be.

With my typing qualification, I got a job typing at British Rail, in London, in the Complaints Department. I enjoyed the job. However, the problem was, it took me two and a half hours to get there and two and a half hours to get home. I was spending far too much time travelling, so I applied for another job in London, working as a legal typist at the Board of Trade in Fleet Street.

Unfortunately, my typing was not accurate enough to deal with the intricacies of legal documents, so I decided to move to another job. This was easy in London during the sixties. I applied for and got a job at the Electrical Association for Women, as a trainee secretary.

I loved the job because during the interview I asked them if I could have an hour and a half for my lunch break so that I could play netball and swim and my interviewer, who later became my manager, Mrs Pickford, granted my request. She was a lovely lady, and we got on really well.

I was welcoming to everyone who came in, and I would do anything I could to help. She loved my 'can do' attitude. The job entailed quality testing electrical equipment; I remember the most unusual test was allowing old ladies to keep checking out the heated toilet seat we had installed in the basement toilet.

In my hour and a half lunch break, I often went to Lincoln Inn Fields and played netball with some ladies in the Kent County team. The standard was quite high. There was a swimming pool nearby too, so when I was not playing netball, I was swimming.

As I worked in the city, I was able to have lunch with my Uncle Mike. He was a retired Squadron Leader from the Royal Air Force. He worked in the Royal Bank of England. I had lunch with him a few times and chatted about his many adventures as a pilot.

Uncle Mike and Aunt Celia were aware of the terrible time I had had at home, so they invited me to their house at Hill Rise, Garston, Hertfordshire, where I stayed for many happy weekends.

My Aunt Celia was a small, beautiful, and wise lady who made me very welcome. She gave me a bedroom upstairs and told me I was welcome to stay whenever I wanted. I felt so loved there, that writing this brings tears to my eyes.

From the very start, Aunt Celia started educating me in basic things. She showed me how to set a table, have good manners, to eat correctly and how to behave well. My Uncle Mike only had one rule 'No horsing around in the house, do it outside'. Their home was beautiful but not precious, it was very warm and comfortable.

When I arrived on a Friday afternoon, there was always a smell of home-made pies. They were kept in a cupboard under the stairs to cool and we would eat them over the weekend.

To this day, I make apple pies with my beautiful grandchildren using the same recipe as Aunt Celia. Both my uncle and aunt showed me great kindness and taught me to have self-respect and respect for others. They also gave me an insight into what family stood for.

Aunt Celia was very calm and patient. We spent many hours shopping together, having great fun trying on clothes. As well as a trained hairstylist, Aunt Celia was a seamstress, and she would ensure that my clothes fitted well and take up hems to keep me in fashion.

It was the time of the miniskirts. She taught me how to put in perm rods and I did her hair every six months or so. They had travelled the world in the RAF, and they often sat with me at night reminiscing about the good times they had experienced.

It was on one such night that Uncle Mike told me about the Women's Royal Air Force.

"They offer reasonable pay and a uniform," he said. "Including PKs." (passion killers—a huge pair of knickers). I was sold on the idea, but I was far too young to join, as the minimum age to enlist was eighteen and I was still only sixteen.

However, at this point, I knew what I wanted, so I put a plan in place. Sadly, Uncle Mike and Aunt Celia passed some years ago. I loved them both dearly, and I still miss them to this day.

Airforce Adventures

I wanted to join the WRAF (Women's Royal Air Force), but I did not have anywhere near enough qualifications, so I decided to go to night school at Deptford Community College to study maths and English. I also took maths and English correspondence courses.

During my night classes, I met the college PE teacher who was arranging outward bound expeditions. He invited me to an expedition at Burwash Outward Bound Centre for a weekend, so off I went. I had a terrific time.

Whilst I was there, the principal asked me if I could help in the summer holidays. I agreed and for a week I taught the children to canoe, helped them with orienteering, fitting lifebelts, making food and whatever else was required.

The lifesaving qualification I took previously enabled me to work with the children who were learning to canoe. During the week, I also achieved a basic canoe coaching certificate. The week was such an enjoyable and rewarding experience I continued to pursue these activities for many years.

It was 1964, and I was seventeen. I was still too young to join the WRAF. It was time to pursue another adventure. I learned that there was an opportunity to go grape picking in France, plus other seasonal work available.

The Auberges de Travailleurs in French cities had information on temporary work. I joined the Youth Hostel Association to access reasonably priced accommodation, bought a 10-gear bike with panniers and a plane ticket from Lydd to Le Touquet. I packed my panniers with underwear, one dress, toiletries, socks, a plastic plate, a cup and my sleeping bag. I was ready to go.

What an experience. The roads were easy to follow into Paris until I hit the Champs-Élysées. I rode up the Champs-Élysées to the Arc de Triomphe. At the Arc, I got stuck in the twelve-lane roundabout. There was so much traffic, everyone was blowing their horns and I was unable to get off at any of the twelve exits.

I went round twice, until eventually a police officer could see that I was struggling, so he kindly stopped the traffic and helped me on my way. I am certain that without out his assistance, I would be there still.

It took a few days to get to the Mediterranean. It was no hardship. The French people were very friendly and made fabulous food; the French bread, fresh every day with cheese, ham, and bananas, was to die for.

I cycled to Toulon in the South of France. I could not believe my eyes; when I saw the Mediterranean for the very first time, I just had to jump into the sea. At night, every movement created phosphorous lights. I could not wipe the smile off my face.

However, I was not there for a jolly holiday. I was there to work. I found my way to the employment exchange and asked about jobs. Picking grapes in the South of France is extremely hard work, but it paid well, £11 a day plus board, food and one litre of wine daily. I started work at 6am had breakfast at 9am for half an hour, worked to 12.30 and then, as is customary in France, had a two-hour lunch break, then went back to work until 5pm.

The work was so hard because in the South where we were, the grapes were Muscat grapes. They grew in very low bushes, so it was back-breaking work, and I got stung by bees every day for ten days. But I did it. Thank God for the wine.

After eating tea and sharing wine with the other workers, I could hardly keep my eyes open. I met so many people, some from the Sorbonne Université and some backpackers on adventures like me. It was a great experience, and I made great friendships. I stayed in a youth hostel and loved swimming in the

Mediterranean Sea.

A few weeks later, I moved on to Perpignan and packed peaches. Wow! The fresh, chilled peaches were absolutely delicious. It was an early start, 5.30am through to 9am. This was followed by a half hour break and then work until 11.30am. We were told that we could eat as many peaches as we liked. Suffice to say, that if I see a peach now, I cringe.

We got paid enough and stayed in a youth hostel. The last stint before the season was over was grape picking in Lyon. This time the grapes were on a vine, so no bending, thankfully. The money was still good, and the food was fantastic. Six courses on one plate, unlimited fresh bread, wine and even schnapps; I slept well.

Eventually, it was time to take my entry test for the WRAF and I couldn't wait. I wanted to teach physical education, inspired by my earlier experience with Ms Patel, the PE teacher. I never thought I could be a PE teacher, as I had so little education. I'd never get into college, but I decided to go on a mission to find a way to teach and get paid at the same time.

"I can do it," I told myself constantly those days. I was so happy to be able to join the WRAF, but I refused to sign up if I couldn't train to be a Physical Training Instructor (PTI). It was an unusual request, but it was granted.

Whilst I was on my PTI training in South Wales, I got my qualifications to go deep. I was invited to go on a sub Aqua expedition to Malta. I was so happy. Off we all went to dive in the Mediterranean Sea. All our equipment was supplied, the tanks filled and with my training in a quarry, I now was now ready to dive in this magnificent, clear, blue sea.

Down I went to 60-feet on my monitor. I could see the people's legs swimming above clearly, as if they were beside me. I felt comfortable and safe just like all the fish swimming around me. It's something I will never forget. We did different dives every day. I felt great joy being amongst such colourful beauty.

When I was posted to Germany, I asked the department head if I could organise an expedition to Sardinia so other ladies could also experience what I had in the Mediterranean. It was granted, so we camped for 10 days, walked the hills, snorkeled, went water skiing and swimming. It was a great success filled with fun experiences and created fantastic memories.

In 1965 I joined the WRAF. I loved my initial training enormously. I learned how to march, how to spit and polish shoes and take great care of the uniform. I felt proud to march in the 'passing out parade'.

I was sent to RAF Cosford to pass some time until my PE course started. This posting was extremely eventful. I got sent for boxes—the cricket team joke. I was also sent for 'a long stand', another joke. It was a training station for cadets, and the facilities were excellent with a swimming pool, diving boards and a trampoline. I took advantage of it all.

Image courtesy of Paula Tatters.
Gymnastic Display Team - Royal Air Force at Earls Court, London.

Image courtesy of Paula Tatters.
Gymnastic Team Toured Britain.

After being introduced to their trampoline, my sergeant saw me and asked if I would try high-board and spring-board diving. I was then able to join the diving, trampolining, and swim relay teams.

Finally, I was off to St Athan in South Wales for my physical training course. I was so excited I could hardly contain myself. Here I was going to be educated so I could teach sport. Me! With only 2 years and 9 months of formal education.

I learned all about the body, like how it moves, strength training, the rules of all the popular sports and how to referee them. We were also introduced to scuba diving. We trained in a quarry where the water was very deep. I got my PADI qualification, so I could do deep dives. The exploration of another world was magic. It was a pure joy.

Image courtesy of Paula Tatters - Synchronised Trampolining.

My experiences so far had enabled me to achieve and enjoy the success I had. Due to my excellent and conscientious PE teacher who took me to netball all over the county, I was good enough to get into the WRAF team. My lifesaving award and experience at Cosford enabled me to qualify as an Amateur Swimming Association teacher and because I had practised diving at Cosford, I also got picked for the WRAF team.

I also loved to run and got selected for the WRAF athletics team. My dreams were being realised, and now I had a job I loved.

Image courtesy of Paula Tatters.
Paula awarding Her Majesty Queen Elizabeth II a 60th birthday present (Pewter candle sticks for her private chapel) on behalf of the WRAF.

I was chosen to represent the WRAF in many sports and was sent to train in Cyprus and Malta. I was beside myself with happiness. My time was divided between netball and athletics.

I was being paid to be an athlete and to play netball. I was a professional sports person!

Once the work was over, it was time to play. 'The Prison' in Cyprus was a great nightclub. I was the first person to rock up wearing 'hot pants'. I was asked on the last night if I would donate my 'pants' so they could frame them and display them at the entrance to the club. I declined, but it sure did make me smile.

After training, my first post was to RAF Halton, not too far from London. It was a training camp for nurses and dental hygienist. My role was to help to keep them fit. The head of my department looked at my records and promptly sent me to the education centre.

"If you want to progress, then you must get more education," he said. It was excellent advice, as shortly after I completed my education, I got promoted to Sergeant. With that came the posting I had requested; it was to the Rehabilitation Unit at RAF Chessington, which was now a Tri-Services Rehabilitation Unit. It was the first time that the RAF Army and Navy had trained together.

There were twenty-seven weeks of intensive medical training. When I was on my initial training for PTI in Wales, I had visited the unit on a tour and knew what it was like. So, when I was accepted there, I was ecstatic.

The training was extremely intense. I had to know every muscle, how it worked, what bone it was attached to, and where on the bone it was attached. I often woke with parts of the skeleton in my bed. Passing the exams meant I was qualified to help people to recover from injuries. What a fun place to work; everyone made the effort to be happy.

It was wonderful to help people who were injured, teach them how to walk again, and teach them how to get stronger. I really, really loved the job. I was also the PTI for the station, so I arranged netball matches and trained girls to get fitter.

I helped people recover from their injuries, be they returning from war, or in service for their country. I also had in my class professional football players and even the Combined Services hammer thrower, a huge man with a hand injury.

Also in the medical class, one serviceman had been accidentally ejected by a seat from a static plane to hit the roof of the hanger with such a force he had serious head and body injuries. To see the improvement as he progressed was heart-warming for him and his family.

There was a structure to all the classes working with doctors and physiotherapists. My favourite was helping men and women recover from leg and knee injuries. It was such fun having a loud music warm up with everyone sitting on the floor. Specific quadriceps exercises made them stronger.

Then the fun began with floor volleyball. It was so competitive, it was just fun, fun, fun. Helping an injured person walk and seeing the joy on their faces was magic.

It was here that I met and fell in love with an REME engineer (Royal Electrical and Mechanical Engineers). We got married and moved into a flat in Leatherhead, very close to Chessington.

Early in our marriage, my husband attended a three-week Army training course. When he returned home, while we were reading mail in bed, he turned pale.

"What's wrong?" I asked. He showed me the letter. It was from some lady saying how much she missed him. Really, we had only been married for six months.

So, we talked and decided that his indiscretion was just a mistake, and it wouldn't happen again. This was fine with me. I was able to let it go. However, he could not or would not let that be the end of it.

From that day, every man I spoke to, or who put their arm around me, resulted in a line of questioning. He wanted to know everywhere I went. He had become unbelievably jealous of me, thinking I was going to have an affair as revenge.

It was around this period that I was competing at athletic meetings. I was winning regularly, and people gave me hugs to congratulate me. To him, this became increasingly problematic.

Then he got posted to Germany. I had moved on from his fling, so I applied and got posted to the RAF Headquarters at Rheindahlen to be with him. I had hoped a change of surroundings would alter his attitude. Unfortunately, after a couple of months, I realised he had not changed, and I eventually stopped loving him.

It was around this time I got a call from my dad to say that my sister Deidra had died. He asked me if I would take my mum to the funeral.

My sister was living in the USA at the time. I went to collect my mum from London, and we flew to Chicago. We were met by my cousins, who wanted me to choose a coffin for my sister. Once I had made my selection, Mum, and I went to the funeral home.

My sister was laid out, beautifully dressed, hair done, with makeup on. I could not believe it. She was only twenty-two. My mother was so distraught, she tried to lift her out of the coffin. It took all my strength to stop her.

I looked at my sister laying there, and I made the decision, there and then, that I was going to change my life. I was not happy and didn't want to have children with my husband. Then I went home to Lewisham and informed my dad that I was going to leave my husband and file for divorce.

Once I returned to Rheindahlen, I told my husband I was going to divorce him, then I moved into the Sergeant's Mess. I wanted to be free and have fun without having to look over my shoulder. My request for a posting back to Chessington was granted. It was the camp where I felt most at ease.

I loved helping people to recover and rehabilitate, but most of all, I wanted to put smiles on their faces. The first day back, I saw a guy in the Mess. I thought he was picking up something from the floor and thought to myself 'they have very young cleaners here now'.

When I asked him for a serviette for my meal, I received a retort.

"Who does she think she is? The Queen?" he said. Later that evening, I was invited to a friend's birthday and someone's going away party. I walked into the Mess, and I saw the very same 'cleaner'. He was a Sergeant, and it was his leaving party. He looked me up and down.

"You are not bad for a WRAF," he had the cheek to comment. I had just met Graham Tatters.

Graham was leaving that weekend to start his aircrew operational conversion to Nimrods at RAF St Mawgan in Cornwall. We had had fun at the going away party, so when he invited me to go to St Mawgan for a visit, I accepted.

I took the train to Newquay, where he picked me up. I had a wonderful weekend. We danced for hours in the Sergeant's Mess. I travelled down several times after that and always had a great time.

On one occasion when we got back to the flat that he was sharing with a friend, the funniest thing happened. We were on a pull-down bunk bed that folded into the wall. Unfortunately, it was not made for two adults. With both of us on it, the top bunk folded back into the wall, jamming us upside down against the lower bunk. It was hilarious. We couldn't stop laughing, and it took us almost half an hour to extricate ourselves.

Once we were vertical again, I told him I was joining the airlines. It was late at night, but we talked into the early morning, discussing what our next step would be. He was of the opinion that I would probably meet a pilot and that would be that. I said that if our relationship was going to last, then it was going to last.

We decided to see what the future would bring. He drove me back to Bodmin and I caught the train to Paddington. Only time would tell what our future would hold.

Getting My Wings

Getting back to RAF Chessington, where I loved helping people to recover from horrific injuries. It was magic. Unfortunately, the second time round, it was not nearly as enjoyable as many of the staff I had worked with previously, had moved on.

Plus, my own personal circumstances had changed. I decided I had to have a change of career and I remembered my cousin I had met at my sister's funeral who was an air hostess with an American-based airline. We talked for hours about her travels, the job, and the fantastic places she had been to. It sounded really exciting and after the trials and tribulations of the previous seven months, I thought it would be a great way to move on.

Initially, I thought about joining the aircrew in the RAF as an Air Load Master, but a chance comment at a party changed that. I was at a party, chatting to friends, and I told them I was considering joining the aircrew in the RAF. One of my friends asked if I had considered becoming an air hostess with a civil airline; another chipped in and in jest, said that I would never get a job like that.

That was like a red rag to a bull; six weeks later, at the age of twenty-six, I was out of the WRAF. It was 1973, and I was starting a six-week intensive course with British Caledonian Airlines.

Gone was the illusion of just serving up tea, coffee, meals, and drinks. That was part of it, but the emergency drills, crash drills, evacuation drills, numerous health and safety training sessions, and how to manage passengers, made up the majority of the course.

I found the entire experience wonderful, and I was thrilled when I passed. Then again, maybe it was just because I loved the uniform. I felt really smart in my Stuart clan tartan kilt. We were even given guidelines of what make-up to wear that suited the red and blue tartan.

Being part of the British Caledonian Team was such a thrill; I could not believe my luck. I had just left a career where I was paid to do sport and loved every minute. Now I was being paid to be happy and smiling every day, wearing a different uniform, and travelling the world.

Upon receiving my first schedule, I was amazed; the principal routes were Los Angeles -11 hours flying, and then 5 days off; New York - 8 hours flying, and then 3 days off and Jamaica - 9 hours flying and then 5 days off. Every month, this was going to be my work; I thought I had died and gone to heaven. It was mind blowing.

Because everything was new to me, I always found different things to do and places to see on every trip. I was not one for sitting by the pool with the crew and chilling with a few drinks. The number of times I went to Disneyland, I could have been a tour guide.

There was this Haunted House where you got into a lift that had pictures on the walls. Those pictures stretched as we descended underground, and the people were sitting on one another's shoulders. The lower we went, the longer the pictures became. We were then transported in these high-backed pod chairs through a very dark and spooky atmosphere.

I was amazed at the length of time a ride could take. There was the Pirates of the Caribbean boat ride through tunnels, under waterfalls. Throughout the ride, pirates jumped out when least expected.

My favourite place was up the Swiss Family Robinson tree. It was huge; every leaf individually pressed and stuck onto the huge branches which were four floors high.

Everything that was needed for the family, all that they had in the film, was there. Even a pulley to lift water cups and the water for cooking and washing. All the children's beds and the cot were in place; it was so well done.

On the transport into the park, a recorded message from Walt Disney was played. He told us how he built this park so visitors would be unaware of the outside world, and that was exactly how it was. Everyone was so happy; it was a glorious place to visit, which I did on very many occasions.

New York

What can I say about that city? It was just fantastic. There were so many skyscrapers, the number of which was only superseded by the number of taxis. I could not believe there would be enough people to warrant so many, but they always had passengers, and even more people hailing them.

Day and night, the traffic never stopped. It was bedlam with car horns blowing, often for no particular reason that I could see. It seemed that everyone was in a hurry to get somewhere.

The hotel that the crew stayed in was right in the middle of NY and our hotel was just two blocks away from where my Uncle Ger and Aunt Josie lived. They had often visited my family in Lewisham, and I had always been very comfortable in their company.

So once again, I did not hang around with the crew in the hotel. I visited with Ger and Josie. They always had a bacon sandwich ready when I arrived and a bed for the night.

It was during one such visit that my Remedial Therapist training at RAF Chessington came in very useful. My aunt had hurt her leg in a road traffic accident and was really struggling to walk. The medical treatment she had received was not great, so when I visited, I showed her exercises to strengthen her leg.

I must have learnt something in my training, because eventually I got her walking. This allowed me to spend time with her in the city. On every stop-over we would go to Macy's, an enormous department store. We would have a coffee and then trawl the departments with discount bargains.

There were always deals on the most beautiful soft towels. I bought them as presents for all my family and friends. I enjoyed looking around the huge store with its bargains in the basement; the first-floor perfumery; the second-floor lingerie; and third-floor crockery. I would remember these floors later in my life and incorporate them into my exercise routines!

My flying schedule also included some short haul UK and European flights and some standby days when it was just potluck. Imagine ending up on a long haul to Brazil. The crew's hotel was facing the Copacabana Beach and with an eight-day stop-over, I was ashamed to call this work.

It is one of the places I would love to go again. The beach was just awesome, packed full of the most beautiful people. I went to see the massive statue of Christ the Redeemer, then on to Sugarloaf Mountain. I walked and swam every day. I just could not take my eyes off people of all ages; they were so elegant, so fit looking and so strong.

There were non-stop volleyball games the length of the beach. Ipanema was the next beach along and remembering the song I just had to visit it. If I thought Copacabana Beach was something special, then Ipanema was even more so.

One day I took a ferry across to an island just off the point of Mount Lerene. The passengers tapped the deck rails with a samba beat as we crossed. There were no vehicles allowed on the island, so the only transport was bicycles. It was a fantastic experience to cycle around this beautiful island with no awful exhaust fumes filling the air. The journey back to the mainland was once again accompanied by the passengers drumming and humming to the samba beat.

One of the perks of being an air hostess was that you could take any family member on a British Caledonian flight at 10% of the normal fare. I decided to make the best of this opportunity and to take my mum to New Zealand.

One reason for going there was to visit my brother Desmond's family, my dad's brother and his family, which included numerous cousins. We had ten beautiful days together, after which I had to return home, but my mum stayed on for another twenty days.

Hilda, my sister, and I also took a flight to Nairobi in Africa. I'd already been there, so when we arrived at the airport, we jumped on a bus to Mombasa. What a journey it was travelling with all the locals. It was a terrific ride. We shared the bus with the chickens and even a baby pig.

The people were just so friendly. We hadn't been prepared for such a long journey, so when the other passengers recognised our oversight, they kindly offered to share their food with us. They were all so lovely and kept smiling at us.

The driver was also aware of our tourist status, so he would slow down whenever we approached wild animals. We saw elephants, giraffes, and monkeys all roaming free. We had been unsure about travelling by bus, but now we realised what a great decision we'd made. It was far better than being stuck on a train.

In Mombasa, we stayed at the White Sands Resort where the accommodation was first class; the food was excellent, and the service was first rate. The only negative of the trip was that every night Hilda would stand on a chair and wait until I had checked that there were no spiders in the room, or more importantly, in the bed.

I had to strip the bed back before she would step down from the chair. It was the same rigmarole every night, but I never found a spider. I was pleased she didn't mind the small lizards, because they were everywhere.

We could not visit Africa without going on a safari, so we booked a day trip. It was a 3.30am start; just the two of us and our driver in an open top jeep. No one could have told us what an experience we were about to live through. It was a trip of a lifetime, seeing lions, elephants, rhinos, crocodiles and so many species of birds that we lost count; all in their natural habitat.

We drove for hours, and we realised why we had such an early start–the animals were all up and about before dawn. They were obviously used to visitors as they showed no signs of being disturbed by us. They just looked at us as if saying, "Hi, nice to see you."

We had a fantastic ten days, but it just flew by. It seemed we had only just got off the bus when we were boarding the train back to Nairobi airport. We boarded at 8pm and had dinner at 9pm. The trip was like being back in the colonial days. The dinner was full silver service, really up market and wonderfully comfortable.

When we returned to our cabin, the huge double bed had been unfolded with the covers turned back. At dawn, as we were having breakfast, the train slowed to allow the passengers to view all the wild animals which were just waking up. When we returned to our room, the bed was folded away, and everything was immaculate. It was a marvellous trip and one I will never forget, and to have shared it with Hilda was extra special.

Hilda also came with me to Los Angeles. However, this time I was working. I was on an eight-day turnaround, so we went to Disneyland and to visit our cousins in San Diego. Hilda had always wanted to be a hairdresser, but she had never had the opportunity in London. The cousins told her about a cosmetology school in San Diego, so she took the plunge and stayed to study hair and beauty.

I guess I had been born lucky, as one of my other standby call outs was a flight to Singapore with a three-day stopover in Bahrain. I had never visited the Middle East, so I was really excited to go there. My crew were scheduled to return to the UK, and another crew was to take our aircraft on to Singapore.

Both crews were invited to go to the Sheik's palace for a party. Luckily, I had packed a dress good enough to attend a party so off we went. The marquee at the palace was unbelievable. How exciting, going to a palace. We were wined and dined in an enormous tent, and we had a great time.

During a visit the bathroom, I happened to speak to a hostess who was on the crew going to Singapore. We chatted for a while; she was saying she was going to be in Singapore over Christmas, whereas her boyfriend would be in London. My brain started working overtime, as Graham was in Singapore with an RAF detachment. So, as the saying goes, 'opportunity knocked'.

“What does a hostess have to do to swap flights?” I asked. It was just before Christmas, and I was going back to an empty flat in London. The hostess smiled and took very little persuasion to swap flights with me. But that was the easy part. I needed to get permission for the swap.

I asked a waiter if I could make a phone call. As I was waiting for a response, to my great surprise, the Prime Minister of Bahrain had overheard my request and came and introduced himself to me. He escorted me down a multitude of long corridors to his office in the palace. I phoned the head office in London and was put through to operations.

I gave a sob story, laid it on thick about Christmas, the season of goodwill, and the joy that the man on the other end of the phone could give to two people. Then I explained that the hostess and I were at the same experience level and eventually, although rather reluctantly, he sanctioned the swap.

The deed was done, so all I had to do now was to arrive in Singapore and find Graham. That should be easy, compared to the deal I had just achieved, I thought.

I was on standby flight to Singapore and excited as I had not been there before. Unfortunately, there was bad turbulence and a lot of people were sick. I collected the sick bags from my area and disposed of them into a garbage bag.

On the way back down the isle, I saw a woman in floods of tears.

"Are you ok? Can I help you," I asked. She shook her head.

"My teeth were in the sick bag," she said and opened her mouth to show me. "I am going to see my family I don't want them to see me like this, and all upset."

I went back to the rubbish bag where the sick bags were, and pulled them out. I pressed gently on each one until I found the bag with her teeth in. After washing them, I took them back to the lady. She was ecstatic and told my senior person she was delighted. She thanked me with the biggest smile.

Singapore is not a large place, and there was only one RAF camp left on the island. I phoned RAF Tengah and got a message to the maritime ops desk to tell Graham I was in the Hyatt Hotel in

Singapore City.

Rat-a-tat-tat sounded on the door. When I opened it, there was Graham smiling like the cat who got the cream. His lips were covered in cold sores. Stuff it, I thought. I don't care. We gave each other an enormous hug. To spend Christmas in Singapore was a great surprise and certainly fabulous, but I did cry a little on Christmas Day as it was too hot. Christmas is supposed to be cold and preferably snowing. I didn't cry for long, though.

I had four glorious days in Singapore before I had to fly back to Bahrain. When I got to Bahrain, I was told to stay on the aircraft and report to the head office upon landing at Gatwick. I was severely scolded and told in no uncertain terms that if I did anything like that again, I would be asked to leave. After about eighteen months flying, I decided it was time for another change of career.

Scotland to America

It was 1974, and it was time for Graham and me to move forward together. When Graham was posted to Kinloss, we decided we wanted to live outside the airbase. We wanted the continuity of schools for our children we hoped to have soon, and wanted to be part of a community.

Stuart wanted the same experience for our children, as he had enjoyed, of growing up in a close community. Not surprisingly, my son Stuart now wants the same for his children and has moved into a house just across the road from ours. His children attend the same school as Graham did.

We bought a house in Elgin, Scotland and prepared to move in. I needed to find a job. A friend told me that there was a position available at Gordonstoun School to teach Physical Education. The school is quite close to Elgin, so I decided to apply. I sent my CV along with all the coaching qualifications I had taken when I was in the WRAF.

Whilst I was visiting Graham, I phoned the headmaster to see if he would like to interview me, as I was in the area. Remember, I left school before I was fifteen, with only an RSA in Typing, and here I was applying for a job at the very same school that His Majesty King Charles III had attended.

It was, and still is, an exceptionally prestigious school. I was appointed to a part-time post, which I held from 1974 to 1997. I worked there for twenty-three years, two afternoons each week, teaching hockey, netball, badminton, swimming, squash, athletics and tennis.

I loved the job and was able to accompany the students to competitions all over the north of Scotland. The scenery in the countryside in this part of Scotland is stunning. Driving through it in the school's big, yellow minibus, no matter what the season, gave me great pleasure.

Once I started doing the exercise to music, the school asked me to do it for the girls. It went so well that it continued for a few years. The students loved the step class with its loud and modern music. It was a great workout. Amazing exercise for all levels of fitness as the step height was adjustable.

The school liked the classes so much they offered to buy them off me when I left. I loved the job and was able to accompany students to squash competitions all over northern Scotland. The scenery of the countryside was, and still is, stunning, and driving through it no matter what the season, gave me such great pleasure.

I also applied for a job at the local swimming pool as I was qualified as a lifesaving coach and Amateur Swimming Association teacher. I worked this around my Gordonstoun job.

Paula's no dumb - bell

If you think training with dumb-bells in a swimming pond is a good way to get drowned, meet Paula Clancy.
Irish colleen Paula is running everyone into the ground on the Highlandd games circuit - thanks to her unusual form of weight training.
She's also winning the high and long jumps.
Paula is a games coach at Gordonstoun school and teaches swimming in the Munro Baths, Elgin.

Back then, every child at school had to learn to swim. During the school term, sixty children were dispersed between the two pools every forty-five minutes. Two areas in the beginner pool and three areas in the big pool.

One of my greatest joys has been to teach people to swim. I started 'Mother and Baby' sessions, helping mothers and babies to be comfortable and have confidence in the water. I also gave lifesaving classes. In a 'swimming for the disabled' class, I had to give the 'kiss of life' to a young child who went blue and could not breathe. The child's mother has stopped me in the street many times since, to give me a hug.

As a qualified trampolining coach, I was asked if I could offer classes in the local community centre. Again, I loved helping children and adults to gain new skills. So, for a few years, I also helped the local youth athletics team. I was most fortunate to live in an amazing town and close to the athletics track and swimming pools.

I also helped Mr Craig, who made canoes, to set up a canoeing club. We trained in the pool and out on the nearby river, which conveniently ran through the local park, offering a degree of safety. Regular picnics added to the pleasure of the sessions.

I also liked make-up and became an Oriflame Beauty Consultant giving advice and helping people to choose colours and apply the make-up. It was fun to do and another skill to learn. All my jobs came in very handy when the mortgage on our house went up to 16%.

I had five different jobs to help to cover our bills. Graham, in the Royal Air Force, could not get a second job, so it was up to me to raise as much as I could. We also rented a room to a very good friend, Colin Birnie, who gave us six months' rent in advance to help us at this difficult time. Forty-three years later we are still in the same family home.

1975

We had been together for over two years now and had a lovely home. Graham and I agreed that we would like to have children, so we decided to get married. We were deeply in love. Fortunately, over forty-five years later, we are still as much in love now as we were then.

Graham told me he married me for my genes; he wanted to have athletic children. With athletic genes from both sides, we did well. We had two beautiful boys, Stuart, and Colin, just two years apart. From early on, we exposed them to many forms of physical and fun experiences.

We took the boys swimming, of course, and one would often travel in the backpack on his dad's back to football matches on Saturdays. As soon as the boys could sit well, we added children's bike seats to our bikes and off we would go. Our adage was that there was no such thing as bad weather, just a bad choice of clothes. If the boys asked to play a sport, the answer was always yes. They played mainly badminton, football, and golf.

Where we live in Scotland, we have snow in the winter, so snow suits and snow boots are a must. I kept spare snow clothing so that if any friend or family visited, we always had something to keep them warm and dry. We were so lucky, as our home was always full of sporting people, and friends and family who played and contributed to great times.

We had the only flat garden on the hilly road. We wanted our children to be able to play in our garden, so we had it flattened. Everyone was welcome to share it, as long as they didn't expect their children to go home with clean clothes. Latterly, floodlights were added for night-time fun too.

When I first arrived in Elgin, I joined the Athletic Club Committee. We convened to discuss the organisation of the Elgin Highland Games. This was an annual and most amazing spectacle of events. It included traditional Scottish dancing, some sword dancing, and unusual events such as 'tossing the caber'—the throwing of a tree trunk.

Other heavy events included 'hammer throw', 'shot put', and 'tug-o-war'. Both men and women dressed in beautiful tartan kilts, often representative of their clans.

During the summer months, highland games took place across the Highlands. I participated in as many as I could and won many prizes; I held the North of Scotland record for high jump for many years. It was great fun. The running events had staggered starts to add greater equality. Good sportsmanship was always displayed.

Graham was an ardent football enthusiast and managed Bishopmill United for many years. He loved the camaraderie and having responsibility for the team. He later became deputy manager, coach and fitness trainer for the Elgin City Football team.

In 1993, they won the Highland League Championship but were disqualified due to a controversial dispute. After their extensive training, it was a harsh blow, but Graham was still very proud of the men; it was a phenomenal achievement. He has devoted many years to the club, including being manager when it was in the Highland League. He is currently the chairman.

Graham, Cecil Jack, and a hard-working board of directors, along with a team of enthusiastic volunteers, have enabled the club to maintain their place in the Scottish league.

Our next-door neighbour, Arthur Milne, who was a joiner, and a brilliant teacher, came over one time. He had made a wooden golf club and said he would be happy to teach Stuart how to swing it. At eight years of age, he was able to join the Elgin Golf Club for £35 and Lossiemouth Golf Club for £15. What a privilege it was to be able to join these two clubs.

I would often go to the course to drag Stuart back as he was out from early morning until 10pm. He always had money for food and loved every minute of it. Stuart decided that he wanted to be a professional golfer. When he was older, he passed enough exams to give him entry to a UK programme.

When Stuart was fifteen years old, we went on holiday to Disneyland in Florida. One day, we also went to a huge golf store to look for and buy a golf club for his good friend John Murray. Stuart was hitting golf balls when a man asked him what he played off.

"Five," he replied. The man was the owner of the store, and extremely impressed with Stuart's swing. He offered to introduce Stuart to his friend, who was the Athletics Director for Florida State University. The meeting was arranged for the following afternoon.

The director suggested Stuart apply for an athletic scholarship. To even be considered, he would need to pass the SAT (Scholastic Aptitude Test). Stuart was overjoyed. He decided he wanted to go to university in the USA.

Fortuitously, I had friends at Gordonstoun School, who, because they have many students from the USA, have teachers who specialise in this exam. When the time came, Stuart received tuition in maths and English and studied the SAT book. He sat the test and passed with a score high enough to earn him an athletic scholarship.

Next, we needed to find a suitable university. I saw an advert in The Times asking for golfers to go to London to be considered for golf scholarships. We went down to London for two days, after which Stuart was offered one full scholarship at the Citadel —a very prestigious military college in South Carolina. Also, a partial scholarship to Pheiffer University, and a private university in Misenheimer, North Carolina.

After some discussion, we settled on The Citadel. Just after we had booked flights, we received a call from the golf coach at The Citadel. Unfortunately, he informed us that Stuart's math score on his SAT was not high enough for him to start immediately on the athletics programme. He would need to wait a year and do more studying and marching; none of us thought that this would suit him much at all.

I contacted the coach at Pheiffer and explained the situation. At the age of eighteen, Stuart was on his way to university in the USA. However, due to the change in details, upon arrival in the USA, the customs would not accept his entry documentation and said he must either return to the UK or go to jail. He was put on the next plane to London where he was met by my cousin Maureen. She took him to the USA Embassy, where the paperwork was changed very quickly, and then he was on the next plane back to the USA. What an experience, but essential as Stuart had to be in class the very next afternoon.

On arrival, he was picked up at the Airport by Skip Chamberlain. What an exceptionally fortunate meeting that was! Craig and Debbie Chamberlain adopted our son in the USA to guide, help him, and love him as their own; we are still friends today and will always be so grateful to them.

Stuart played for Pheiffer, won many competitions, and was subsequently offered a full scholarship. There is a picture of him in the Hall of Fame for Golf. He studied as well as played and practised extremely hard.

He practised every day. I warned him not to overdo it. He told me that when he gets to the seventeenth hole, he looks across the beautiful course and feels that he has died and gone to heaven. Stuart got his degree and wore a kilt under his robe for graduation. We were so proud of him. After graduation, he wanted to become a professional golfer; fortunately, he had sponsorship for one more year.

Graham chose football as his favourite sport and enjoyed going to training camps. He was selected for Aberdeen FC youth trials. Ultimately, he decided to follow his brother to the USA. He went to summer camp at UNC Charlotte, where the coach was extremely impressed with him, and he subsequently got a full scholarship. He lived quite close to Stuart, which was great for us as parents, as when we visited the States, we got to see both of them; they often came home together too.

Clancy's

Hilda, my sister, paid her way through college and finished her training in the USA. She asked to stay with us in Scotland and we were delighted to have her share our home and enjoy some free time after so much hard work.

She was qualified in cosmetology, hair, and beauty and needed a job. It didn't take long to find one. There were over twenty hairdressing salons in Elgin, and she was offered a job at Kenneth's, the best salon in Elgin. This post was part-time so to increase her income, she cut and styled hair for friends and family too. It was one such friend who gave her the chance of a lifetime.

Sandy Buist, our next-door neighbour, and assistant manager at our local bank, was most impressed with his haircut. He helped us to secure a loan to purchase a small-terraced flat which we intended to convert into a salon. Then fate stepped in.

Working at the bank, Sandy was privy to many business opportunities which arose in the town. Two days after we purchased our flat, he called to inform us that a local hairdresser had passed away and that her salon was up for sale. As we had already stretched ourselves to purchase the flat, we didn't know what to do. However, Sandy said he would sort it and true to his word, a week later, my sister and I were the proud owners of our own salon–Clancy's His and Hers Hairstylists; the first unisex salon in Elgin.

The salon needed complete refurbishment, painting, and deep

cleaning. For a month, family, friends, and staff helped in any way that they could. We were extremely lucky with our wonderful staff, two of whom remained with us throughout the 37 years' ownership of Clancy's. June was both professional and trustworthy; she nurtured young stylists and built up a loyal clientele. Hilda trained Jan as a junior stylist, who later blossomed to be manager of our second salon. She subsequently trained new hairstylists. To this day, she still does my hair.

The day before we opened, I discovered we had no rollers. In the era of the 'shampoo and set', this was disastrous. My husband, in his enthusiasm to clear up the rubbish, had thrown out two large bin bags full of rollers. Being short of funds, we scoured the tip looking for them, but to no avail. I was saved by Barclaycard and withdrew the maximum daily withdrawal before hastily setting off to buy rollers. I also had to ask the staff to bring in rollers from home, which, of course, they did. We also seemed to have lost all of it in our bin bags!

Although the initial outlay had used up all our funds, we were full of excitement for our new venture. We decided to use the best products and got an account with Salon Services. We bought Lamaur hair products which were new and advanced. We encouraged high standards of education by offering training to our junior hairdressers through day release at Inverness College—Moray College in Elgin did not offer hairdressing at this time—and we offered in-house training from senior staff.

We also invited trainers from internationally branded companies to train our staff. Hilda admired the Toni and Guy cuts, so set up video training for the juniors.

With our professional approach and service, we quickly expanded our clientele through personal recommendations. It was important that our staff were always courteous and attentive. They were encouraged to smile and treat our customers well. It was also important that they looked good. We had great fun choosing the uniforms from Glasgow and Ireland. They were smart, washable and wearable.

From the day we opened, we tried to give back to the

community. We held charity days and community collections dressed in flowery onesies. We readily contributed to any worthy causes. However, one service, I feel, outweighed the others.

Image courtesy of Hilda Antley - Giving a cheque to charity.

Hilda was asked to help people who had cancer and were losing their hair. This often affected their self-esteem. Hilda took on this service, and we provided a private room where clients could try on wigs. Hilda really cared for these clients, helping them emotionally, with making decisions so they could leave the salon with a smile on their faces and hair on their heads. It was a wonderfully fulfilling service we provided for many years.

Image courtesy of Hilda Antley
Paula, Hilda and ladies in their onesie uniform.

In addition to hair, we also offered beauty treatments. Hilda was qualified to undertake waxing and eyebrow shaping. As we expanded, we rented the property next door. Once the pigeons moved out and it was refurbished, it looked amazing.

We were fortunate to have wonderful therapists and were able to offer top-of-the-range treatments such as our Guinot facial; liked by Princess Diana and other celebrities. My role was that of receptionist; I took appointments, swept the floor, made refreshments, and ensured that everyone was happy. We held meetings to discuss new products and workshops to train new staff. We also offered demonstrations in the community to showcase our products and treatments.

Being a part of Clancy's was like being part of a family; many young girls came to us from a lot of different backgrounds. We prided ourselves on finding and training young ladies to be proud of. We chose those who were warm, friendly, and wanting and willing to help and always with a smile. Our most junior staff were the first to greet and shampoo our clients.

Some of our ladies were elderly and had little contact with other people, so it was important that we made them feel comfortable and that the experience was enjoyable. We wanted to ensure that every client felt special. Many of our trainees have gone on to have great careers and their own salons.

Like Tracey Devine-Smith, who is a multi-award-winning hairdresser and British Hairdressing Awards Hall of Fame member. She is also the Global Ambassador for the haircare manufacturer, Affinage and Global, the Creative Director for the Glamour Hair Salon group in the UAE.

Image courtesy of Paula Tatters.
Hair, Beauty & Fitness Show for Charity.

Tracey started work at Clancy's at the age of fifteen. Hilda encouraged and promoted her natural flair. She was soon cutting hair and not relegated to sweeping up and making drinks; she said that she'd had the best training with Hilda. The camaraderie and fun times we had at Clancy's have fostered lifelong friendships and many of us still stay in touch.

Fitness, Fun & Despair

Whilst visiting friends in London, I got invited to an 'exercise to music' class, run by Cindy Gilbert of Moves Fitness. I was completely blown away; I loved the whole concept; she was on the stage with a big sound system and a microphone pinned to her chest.

She designed routines to each record, and everyone enjoyed it. I chatted to her at the end of the class, telling her how much I enjoyed it and would consider creating similar classes. She said she offered 3-day courses with Moves Fitness and asked if I would like to know more. I grabbed her contact information and undertook the training.

I was convinced that I would be able to do this and with the support (in case of illness of myself or my children) of my friend Liz George and my sister Hilda; we set up Fitness and Fun. Liz was an experienced PE teacher and a great personality. We procured a double-deck record player with a great sound, and, between us, we designed routines.

Hilda loved them too and we had such fun. We started in the Town Hall and offered a free creche. The sessions were very popular and soon we expanded to other nearby villages. In eighteen months, Hilda and I had saved enough to consider having our own fitness centre. With our savings and a bank loan secured against our house, we started another new venture.

Again, we were so fortunate to have the support of family and friends. With their help, we converted a furniture shop into a very modern fitness centre. There was a lot of major construction work required to ensure that the upstairs was capable of taking the pounding of our fitness classes.

The structural engineer advised us that reinforcement was necessary to strengthen the current wooden beams. Access to the premises was a nightmare. The entrance was via a long passage off the High Street, and it was impossible to get mechanical aids though it.

Luckily, we had two amazing builders, Ally and Chico McHardy, who employed a 'can do' attitude. They found fourteen men to help to manoeuvre four massive steel beams into the building and into place. Further beams were to be jacked up and welded to the four cross beams. It was a tremendous task that few would have attempted, let alone accomplished.

Upstairs, we made a dance studio with nineteen metres of mirrors; this is where we ran the 'exercise to music' classes, step classes and many child development classes. I took on a Tumble Tots franchise and delivered physical development programmes for pre-school children. There were classes for mums with children up to age 2 (who could walk), age 2-3 years and age 3-5 years.

The classes helped children to build balance and physical skills as well as promoting confidence through a wide range of activities using a great selection of equipment and action songs. Joyce Clarke and Trudi Birnie were my star instructors. A wonderful gym instructor, Ivan Scott, also introduced us to the Fit Kids program for children between age 5 and 9. He worked with us on Saturdays and one evening each week.

Downstairs we had a fully equipped gym with two encumberment bikes. We catered to a wide range of fitness levels. We had an easy to program stepper and weights section, which was great for circuit classes. A man I had worked with in the rehabilitation centre in Chessington, Gary Swan-Brown, became our first manager and delivered 'exercise to music' classes. We also wanted to have a health food bar and a social area.

In a lucky turn of events, as I was crossing the road to our hair salon, I bumped into one of our clients–Lesley Atkinson. She asked how the fitness centre was progressing. I told her about the health food bar and that we were looking for someone to run it.

Her daughter, Trudi, had just finished college, and this would be the perfect job for her. She was also perfect for us; she was eighteen years old, very capable, and always smiling. She made fresh salads, jacket potatoes, and home-made soup. The health food bar was ready to go. She remains a family friend. We also recruited Mandy, who was stylish, smart, and welcoming. She was the perfect receptionist. We sold fitness clothing and trainers, too.

Tragedy Strikes

One day, when I was working in the gym in the afternoon, I was called home. I walked into my lounge, and I was told that my young son Colin, aged only four, had drowned at the beach. I was in utter disbelief. I let out the loudest yell and fell to the floor. My beautiful son.

Poor Stuart was sat there; he was only six years old and had lost his baby brother. I had so many questions–how? Why? Against advice, I went to the mortuary; I had to see him.

The news was like a dagger to the heart for my husband. He was broken. I could hardly breathe at the funeral. The pain and hurt were so unbearable. The loss never leaves, and nothing could ever hurt me as much again, ever.

I walked around in a fog. My family and friends were there for me, but they remained outside the fog of grief. How did other people cope? What about mothers during and after the war? How did they survive and continue on with their lives?

All happiness and joy were gone from our home. A noise was missing. Graham and I talked. We did not want Stuart to be an only child. We would try to bring some joy back, to have something to look forward to. I considered never going to the gym again, but that would only achieve more pain and sorrow and letting people down; employees who worked so hard.

I gave myself a talking to. I had to stay strong and do everything possible to make sure Stuart was loved and cared for. Losing a child is so profoundly life changing. I thought 'There must be help and information out there', so I went to the library. But reading about someone else's grief only made me want to die myself. How do people cope? On my way out, I noticed a leaflet with the title 'Compassionate Friends'. I took it home and called the help number. It was a peer support group for bereaved parents. I cried and cried and cried; I had found some help.

I was put in touch with a lady who had also lost her child in a drowning accident, but in a garden pond. We spoke and cried and spoke and cried. She was my light.

"Nothing will ever make it better; you only learn to cope," she said. I also received a small booklet about how other people coped; sharing the pain was good for me. The booklet held lifesaving information; about different phases, knowing you are not alone.

Every Thursday, I took out Colin's pictures and sat and cried on my bed. I have since been a friend to other parents who have lost a child and joined local meetings. One of the things I have pointed out to people is that the first year you just survive. All anniversaries, you just survive. At Christmas, you just survive. There is no joy to be found anywhere. You are just broken.

Graham and I wanted to do something different that we could try to enjoy as a family. We talked about horse-riding and so we went on a Sunday together. Susan and Ally McHardy invited us for bacon sandwiches; these friends were very kind. Stuart wanted a bike, but we wanted to wrap him in cotton wool. We pushed through that fear, and he got the bike!

I decided to offer some exercise classes to keep my brain free from pain. Soon, I found out that I was pregnant–Stuart would not be an only child. I continued to teach the classes up to the two weeks before delivering Graham junior.

When I went into labour, I was admitted to the local hospital in Elgin, but my contractions were not progressing as well as expected and I was transferred by an ambulance with blue flashing light all the way to Aberdeen Royal Infirmary.

It was over eighty miles away. I was quite delirious when I

arrived at the delivery suite, but conscious enough to hear the midwife say that maybe a caesarean section should be considered.

Through my semi-conscious haze, I screamed to be allowed to try one more time. My request was granted, and my new, beautifully strong and healthy baby boy was delivered. We will never replace Colin, but Graham gave us some joy, some noise back in our home, something to look forward to and most importantly, a brother for Stuart. I am forever grateful also for the ongoing support from family and friends which we have never been without.

Fitness and Fun classes continued. We expanded our range to include 'Weightguard', a program to help reduce weight, Slimming Club, dance and step classes. Staff training also continued, plus Tumble Tots, Fit Kids, 'exercise to music' and the gym.

My instructors were warm, friendly, patient, and fun. My speciality was pelvic floor exercises. I would take my classes on imaginary shopping trips to Macy's in New York and visit the bargain basement–that is where most of our pelvic floor muscles are. Imagine the first floor–perfumery, hold in your muscles and go to the next floor, still holding in your muscles. Then release back to perfumery, hold then release. This was a practice to be done every day while brushing teeth or waiting for a kettle to boil.

Many women thanked me years later, even the men too, gave me a smile to say, 'they are working'. We also learned all the moves for Michael Jackson's Thriller, taught to us by Beverly from London, who came specially to teach us.

Again, I was grateful to have the most wonderful and highly qualified staff, Sue Taylor, loyal, hardworking, and most joyful, possessing great empathy and professionalism. She ensured our clients became fitter and more confident. We are friends to this day.

Mel Allan was a brilliant dance teacher, so professional and made clients feel so comfortable. It was such a privilege that they decided to be part of our team. We are still friends too. I have great respect and admiration for them both.

I advertised for an 'exercise to music' teacher and had a response from a lady from Australia. She would only agree to come if I would also train her boyfriend to be an 'exercise to music' and gym instructor. I interviewed him too; he was very keen to become qualified and determined to work hard. He was an extremely popular instructor and went on to run his own gym in Australia because of the qualifications he gained at Fitness and Fun. I was very proud of him and of our role in his success.

With the opening of the new leisure centre in Elgin, we lost quite a few of our clients. The Council laid some Italian stones on the High Street and this work blocked access to our facility for months. There was then a problem with the stones, and they had to re-do them, so the problem persisted for quite a while.

As we still owed a lot of money to the bank, when two gentlemen from a local bar asked if they could use our upstairs studio to host local live bands, we jumped at the chance. They also agreed to put in washroom facilities and a bar.

Those were added, plus a stage, but a week before opening, they pulled out. What were we to do? We decided to continue with the band idea ourselves. Our husbands were called in to help. We were now owners of a nightclub.

I had to go to court to get a late licence which involved a great deal of persistence and much persuasion. When I was finally granted the licence, I was congratulated by a senior solicitor who told me that I'd presented a great case.

The night club, which we named 'The Venue', required strong security, and tight control. We had four excellent security guards, and Graham was responsible for booking the bands. He also collected glasses and frequently had his bum pinched, but still smiled most of the time.

Frank, Hilda's husband, ran the bar, stocked it, and staffed it. I did the meeting and greeting at the entrance and collected the money. We also had an amazing cleaner, Mrs Harvey, who ensured that any broken glass was swept up, and the floors were sparkling for all our daytime classes. We opened 9pm to 3am Friday and Saturday.

Sometimes, we had bands sleeping downstairs in the basement. I put out mattresses, quilts and pillows, cereal, tea, and coffee. There was a shower and toilets. We had a famous band from Edinburgh, Big Vern, who was always fully booked. I put on a big spread for them after every show and made them a cooked breakfast in the morning. We had so many bands but never had any trouble.

Running a nightclub, a fitness centre and a hairdressing and beauty salon, plus teaching at Gordonstoun, took up a lot of time. Having support was vital. I had a live-in nanny, Sandra Johnson, who was extremely versatile, unflappable and had a lovely personality. She produced any music I required and when the children went to school, she ran the creche at Fitness and Fun and then the reception.

I also had another lady to do my ironing and cleaning at home, which gave me more time to spend with my children. We sold Fitness n Fun, but we had a plan to do classes in the community and continue with the Tumble Tots programme. We planned to find a hall that would store all our equipment and have a big enough hall for classes every Tuesday morning.

Bishopmill hall in Elgin said yes, so we continued with our walking up to age 2, age 2 to 3, and age 3 to 5. Joyce Clarke, Trudi Birnie, and myself ran the classes. I then had to find a place to take the Step classes. In the end the only place I could find was the physiotherapy department in Doctor Gray's hospital. There was only one problem, I had to move all the equipment before class, and put it all back after class.

One hour each way, but it was worth it. Classes went every Monday and Wednesday evening for 2 hours. The steps were in the van so people collected them and took them back after. We also introduced with our other classes, including line dancing and the baggy T-shirt class. What fun we had with the Baggy T-shirt ladies. We took them walking, singing, hugging trees and doing press ups on school benches.

It really was fun for the summer Kate Sansum from Fitness n Fun joined me and we laughed a lot a great experience. Kate and

Lee her husband who were in the process of setting up their own Kick-boxing facility, understood the benefit of the Tumble Tots programme. She had watched the classes and decided she would like to have it in her new facility. She offered to buy the equipment off us. I was so happy that the whole programme was to be continued.

To this day, ladies who took their children to Tumble Tots say what a wonderful programme it was for the mums as well as all the benefits for their child's development.

We were also blessed with 'The Angel from the North', my mother-in-law, Kathleen Tatters. She arrived with her friend Jack, and Sam the dog, and moved in just a hundred yards from our home. Having a wonderful, loving, and caring granny near us was a godsend.

Hilda's children, and our own, loved her. Hilda's three daughters wanted to call her Gran. She had so much love to share, and nothing was any trouble. She also offered when we were stuck, to cover for us at work, even working with me at the entrance to the nightclub.

Kathleen was so much loved, not just because she made the best chips. She always had something special for her grandchildren and Hilda's children too; she put a smile on all our faces.

Unfortunately, she suffered from the dreaded dementia. We hadn't been able to understand what had changed her from the happiest, funny granny, into someone who upset people. We did not see the signs. Eventually, we took her to our own doctor, who diagnosed her with dementia. Our doctor communicated with her doctor, and she then got the help she needed from a specialist.

We looked after and loved her in her own home until she had to go to a special hospital. Hilda used to go and do her hair and I would paint her nails; eventually, she did not recognise us and has now passed. RIP Kathleen.

We ran 'The Venue' for six eventful years. When we were given an offer that would pay all our bills, give us our sanity back, and some money left over for some fun, we took it.

Out of the Darkness

We had just arrived back from the USA after enjoying a fabulous holiday. Young Graham (our son) was starting at the University of North Carolina at Charlotte and playing for their soccer team.

However, one afternoon, we received a devastating phone call. We were informed that Graham had cancer and was going to see a specialist oncology doctor that day.

Stuart, his brother, saw him the day before, and made him go to the hospital. A young doctor saw him and was concerned about a protrusion on his chest.

Apparently, another senior doctor had said that as he was an athlete, it might be a strained muscle. However, the young doctor persevered with a scan which showed that it was indeed cancer.

The actions of this doctor saved his life, according to the consultant, as the tumour was doubling in size each day. We were informed that it was T-cell lymphoma and that if Graham didn't get chemotherapy immediately, he would be dead in two days.

I boarded the first plane to Charlotte and was with Graham the next day. Craig and Debbie Chamberlain also joined us. Graham had to have a bone marrow operation; Craig accompanied Graham, which was extremely comforting throughout this painful procedure.

On day two, I was told that Graham would have thirty-seven weeks of chemotherapy as there was a nine-pound tumour on his chest which needed to shrink.

Graham was ecstatic that he would be able to play football the following season. This was not to be. The next day, the doctor informed us that the new protocol was a road map for two years of chemotherapy. Graham was utterly devastated; thirty-seven weeks was bad, but two years would mean losing his scholarship.

The treatment was going to cost over $1,000,000 and his insurance only covered $50,000. Fortunately, because he was classed as a child in America, (under 19) we 'only' had to pay ten percent. But we still needed to raise $50,000!

Graham was admitted to The Bloom Clinic. This was a children's hospital with the reception papered in pink balloons, with big comfortable couches and a kitchen which was never empty. It was a fabulous place with welcoming people.

We spent long hours there, sometimes 12-hours a day.

Doctor Mogul was his fantastic doctor. All the doctors were phenomenal and helped to fundraise and we re-mortgaged a property and raised the money as best we could. As the money ran out, a consortium of doctors worked for free. I can never thank them enough.

My son Stuart and his wife Michelle invited us to stay in their house. They had a beautiful little girl, Kylie. Michelle said it was fantastic for her to be able to get to know her granny. That made me incredibly happy and relaxed. I stayed there for six months.

Graham was in the hospital in Charlotte. The first day his brother Stuart came to visit, he had decided to shave his head to support his brother. The most amazing thing was that for the first year, Graham kept all his hair, but the gesture of his brother was much appreciated.

Eventually, the tumour started to shrink, and Graham was allowed to leave the hospital. He lived with Stuart, Michelle and Kylie and visited the hospital each weekday for treatment. He was allowed to eat as much as he liked and he had the most voracious appetite–a Chinese meal on the way home, followed by sushi, followed by prawns and roast chicken, followed by home-made chips at midnight!

With the effect also of the steroids he was on, he barely recognised himself in the mirror. The doctor advised that this was fine, because in the next phase he might not be able to eat.

Sleeping was also a problem, so Graham spent a lot of time on his computer learning about Apple and its latest developments.

He downloaded Apple music, bought Apple equipment for the car, and spent many hours in the Apple store. This whet his appetite for all things Apple, and he is now a specialist engineer working at the Apple head office in California.

Not long after he started getting blasted with chemotherapy, Graham decided he wanted to go running. The mere idea gave me palpitations. I spoke with the doctor, who advised us to let him do what he felt like doing.

Stuart's home was in a cul-de-sac, so it was safe enough to exercise there. Graham could barely put on his clothes or put one foot in front of the other. However, within two weeks, he was able to lift his feet a little more and almost jog.

Some days, the treatment floored him, but whenever he could, Graham would exercise. He then wanted to work out in the gym. Again, the doctor encouraged him. Graham was determined to play football again.

Christmas was about to come; I was having a nervous breakdown, as I still struggled at Christmas time, and still do, from the death of Colin; I was in bits and really struggling to function.

But, at Christmas, to my great joy, my husband Graham was able to join us and our good friends Colin, Trudi and their daughter, Cara. It was a great relief to have such love and support at just the right time. Our families managed to have an amazing Christmas.

The university agreed to let Graham study and train with the team; they said he was fantastic for their morale and that everyone worked harder when he was there. Graham graduated with a degree in Medical Communications and went on to become a professional football player in the USA, Singapore, and Thailand. He became an ambassador for the Lance Armstrong Foundation which helped children with cancer.

I found Lance Armstrong's books uplifting; he had cancer in the brain but went on to win (although illegally) the Tour de France, six times. His journey was so inspirational and, I hope Graham's story gives just as much hope to others.

I felt so fortunate to have met so many loving and supportive people and have such wonderful family and friends.

Hilda also came over and she never left to even go outside the door while supporting me. She also sent for her daughter, Claire, to help. The great joy they gave me brought me out of the darkness.

Bumps & Boobs

Winter 2000

At the age of fifty-three, I had my first experience trying to navigate snow. I took my son Graham, who was fifteen, to Meribel in the French Alps, to learn to snowboard. For me, it was a complete disaster.

Graham received instruction from a French Ski Instructor on snowboarding. I decided to learn to snowboard too. My son went touring with the instructor and I stayed at the bottom of the mountain just trying to slide on the snowboard. I was in a group of six people, all of whom had skied before. So, when they went up the mountain in a gondola, I went with them.

The view was spectacular. I got out of the lift just a short way up the mountain to look at the snow. I was completely blown away by its beauty. I proceeded to clip my boots to the snowboard and slipped a bit. Instead of sliding gracefully, I bounced down the mountain. My son saw me a few times in a heap.

"You don't have to do it, Mum," he said. I was so bad.

"I know," I said in tears. "But I am still going to try." I persevered for two days, even landing on my instructor. A lot.

"This is the closest I have been to any man since I got married," I told him. He laughed at me.

"Well done for trying so hard."

At the end of the day, I did manage a little slide without falling. At midday, I came to the bottom of the mountain to meet my son for lunch. I had it in my backpack. I opened it, looked inside and broke. Huge tears rolled down my face. A lovely French lady came rushing over to me and asked if I was hurt. I told her I wasn't and showed her our squashed-to-a-pulp lunch.

She smiled at me.

"I think you should change to the ski," she said. "It will be better for you. I'm seventy-two and some of my friends are in their eighties and still skiing."

I was relieved. I could imagine how much fun I could still have for many years to come. I did change to skis, but by that time, I had frightened myself. I didn't do too well at skiing either.

However, I loved the chalet, the food was amazing, and I loved the camaraderie of the guests. My son was encouraged to speak French, a wonderful experience for him and a positive contribution to his studies. He toured all three mountains and loved every minute. I was quite determined that despite its tribulations, this would not be my final attempt at snow navigation.

Back in Scotland, I was lucky to live near beautiful beaches, golf courses and be only fifty minutes from our local ski centre - the Lecht. I bought myself some second-hand skis and boots and a bright red all-in-one ski-suit. I was determined to learn.

The nursery slope for beginners was where I decided to start . I grabbed hold of the revolving rope and was pulled up the slope. I made some friends that day who were teaching their four-year-old son to ski. Then I progressed to 'The Eagle', the next level. I loved it; Now I was sliding and not falling.

In 2002, I had a chance to give the Alps another try. Kate's (from Fitness and Fun) mum, Hazel, said that she would come with me on a skiing holiday to Bardonecchia in the Italian Alps. Hazel was a good skier, but she said she would join me in the beginners' class.

We had a lovely instructor, but I was still quite nervous. I was always last in the line as I was petrified that I would send other people to the ground if I were in front of them.

Our instructor was a very patient and smiley man. At least four times every session he would say, "Follow me, follow me". I tried extremely hard, but I was just so bad. Then one time I heard him shouting at me.

"Weight on the downhill ski, downhill ski!" he yelled. At the same time, I heard Hazel screaming.

"You've got it, you've got it!"

The instructor was worried that I wouldn't be able to stop, but I was off; I could ski. I have never looked back. We had so much fun on that first skiing holiday. I also learned that when you come down from the mountain, there is nothing as good as a cold beer or two; then the singing and dancing just follow. Magical times.

Obergurgl

My next skiing holiday was to Obergurgl, a charming village in the Ötzal Alps in Tyrol, Austria: a great place for beginners. This time Hilda and her husband, Frank, came with me. The resort was fantastic and had a bar called The Netherhut, which had live music where we could stop off for a beer on the last run.

Patrons are encouraged to dance on the tables; the first to start gets Schnapps, served on a large paddle to all the people at their table. I didn't need much encouragement. Despite the discomfort of my ski-boots, I did not feel anything except elation!

I also had two friends named Liz, who kept inviting me to go with them to ski in Canada. Again, I had the most fantastic time. We went for ten days to the mountains around Lake Louise. Skiing these mountains was akin to an out-of-body experience; the views, the pristine places and the welcoming Canadian people were literally out of this world.

The most unbelievable day was Liz's birthday. We got to share her exclusive birthday experience of skiing before the mountain was open to the public. There was corduroy-snow–snow just groomed by the snow machine that left tracks all over the mountain that looked like corduroy.

It's an experience called 'First Tracks'. There was only a guide and us on the whole slope. The clear sky, untouched snow and quiet solitude was a truly unforgettable and magnificent experience for which I am so grateful.

This was not to be my last skiing experience in Canada. I returned twice more. I was due to go for the third time in February 2009. However, my life was not all plain sailing. It has been beset with the odd difficulty, and this was to be one such time.

December 2008

Some people say, 'It's all in the genes.' My grandmother had fourteen children; eleven of them had cancer. Because of this, I was on an annual screening program for mammography and colon screening. After one mammogram, I got the dreaded call back. A request to attend the special Breast Clinic in Aberdeen.

My husband went with me to hear the diagnosis, even though he hates hospitals. Once we were both sitting down, the doctor spoke the words no one ever wants to hear. He told me I had breast cancer and that we needed to discuss my treatment plan immediately. I told him he could remove both breasts. My husband nearly fainted.

We left the doctor's office so we could have a quick discussion and get him some much-needed fresh air. I explained to him that as it is hereditary, I didn't want to go through the same treatment twice. I did not want to spend more time worrying about tests and results.

I later found out that I did not have the BRCA gene mutation, which can indicate high risk. However, my decision was made, and I have never regretted it.

We returned to the consultant and confirmed the removal and reconstruction of both breasts. I was diagnosed in December 2008 and had the operation in early January 2009. My concern was that I had a trip to Canada booked in six weeks.

The operation went well; I was very sick from the pain, the drugs, and the morphine. But the vomiting only lasted for a day. On day two, I got up out of bed, but because I had drains on each side of my chest, I had to carry them in pillowcases. I walked round the corridors twice and then rested.

On day three, the doctor came in to see me. I told him about my planned ski-trip to Canada in just over six weeks.

"No chance," he said. I told him that I was fit, and that I healed very quickly. On day four, I proved my point. I walked the corridors again, but I wanted to do more. I looked outside and saw snow on the ground. There was a lovely, tempting garden with benches in it.

I put a blanket around my shoulders, carried my drains in my pillowcases, and walked outside. I did step-ups on the benches. How else would I be fit enough to go skiing in six weeks?

The next day, the physiotherapist came in to give me exercises, but as I was a remedial therapist, I had already begun doing them. She was very pleased and most impressed. I asked if she would have a word with the doctor and tell him how well I was doing.

Having a double mastectomy and reconstruction was not a small operation, but I strongly recommend it. The chances of recurrence are greatly reduced and therefore chances of survival are increased. The body also has greater symmetry, which is a bonus to recovery. There isn't the barrage of worrying tests.

I had one test per year but did not worry unduly. There is no guarantee that cancer will not re-appear, but I certainly feel more reassured. I have had friends who have chosen a lumpectomy or single mastectomy, but they have not survived.

The emotional impact upon husbands is also very traumatic. I believe it is rarely discussed. It can be 'an elephant in the bedroom'. How do you cope with the pain and discomfort? Where can you touch? The scarring and disfigurement are not aesthetically pleasing. It was important to talk. It is not an easy time and requires a lot of love.

Before leaving the hospital, I had a talk with my doctor about my ski-trip.

"No," he said again. So, I continued my physiotherapy and took good care of my large scar and the leaking I had from where the drains had been.

A week before I was due to fly, I had an appointment with my lovely doctor. He gave me a thorough examination–scar, blood pressure, pulse, arm movement and posture. He sat back in his chair, then granted me permission to fly!

"You have done so well. You won't need to take Tomoxifen, " he said. "It's a hormonal therapy often prescribed after mastectomies to reduce the chances of recurrence." Now I could look forward to seeing the snow in Canada.

I stayed in a beautiful complex on an Indian reservation; the Silver Start resort in Kalona; for the second time. This jewel of a ski resort was recommended by our ski instructor at Lake Louise.

The ladies' Canadian ski champion wanted to find somewhere with the same snow as Vail in Colorado, and this was the place. As long as the resort was not detrimental to the surroundings, it was allowed to be built.

Our apartment was in front of the ski lifts, very handy. There was a hot tub at the end of our block, which I went in every night. It only took one beer to be persuaded to do snow angels in my swimsuit!

Enormous thanks to the French lady who in 2000, suggested I swap my snowboard for skis. I'm now in my seventies, and I'm still skiing.

What a Life!

Wow! That's what I think when I look back over the fantastic life I have lived. I have visited and enjoyed meeting people and I've always enjoyed being a free spirit. I am so grateful that I've been able to travel on my own and have visited twenty-three countries to date.

I have always chosen to smile and be willing to help others, no matter what the situation. I believe we have a choice of who we want to be. Being open and approachable is my preference. I've tried to do every task, chore, and job wholeheartedly, and I've sought to improve myself and share any knowledge and skills I had with others.

I have enjoyed motivating others to learn. One of my favourite things is to teach someone to swim who is frightened of the water. I also love helping people to walk after leg injuries. Maybe it is my desire to overcome adversity, which I most enjoy passing on.

Each skill I learned throughout my life opened doors to another opportunity for me. These things did not just happen, they were my choices. At only fifteen years of age, I felt that I was a strong and independent woman, living on my own.

As well as working, I trained to be a lifesaving instructor. This skill and accompanying qualification enabled me to help at the outward-bound centre, which subsequently led to me being able to get a canoeing qualification.

These two qualifications, plus my night school qualification, gave me entry to the WRAF. Prior to my PTI training, I learned trampolining; this led to me representing the WRAF in diving and being part of the RAF gymnastic display team later on down the track.

After being accepted into the RAF gymnastic display team, we were invited to go to Earls Court for the Royal Tournament in London. I with two other girls did a synchronised trampoline display in the arena with thousands of people watching and cheering.

The men did a very fast gymnast display over high boxes timed to perfection. What an amazing experience meeting people from all over the world, and from the joint services Army, Navy, and Airforce. After the tournament was over, we did a tour of Britain. I felt so proud standing outside Earls Court.

I was good enough to also represent the WRAF and captain the joint services netball team.

Another big door opener was choosing to train as a remedial therapist; I can put the letters RT after my name. These qualifications in total led to my appointment as a teacher at the very prestigious Gordonstoun private school.

With my sister's choice of staying to train as a hairdresser in the USA, we were able to set up Clancy's, then the fitness centre and even a nightclub. My desire for education and my determination have enabled myself, and my sister, to train many more people who have gone on to have amazing careers.

My personal circumstances also have enabled me to recognise those who work hard and show commitment and loyalty and I feel I am able to recognise those with personality and drive.

Who would have thought that with only two years and nine months of education myself, that I would have been able to educate others, achieve what I have and enjoy the life I've had?

Six or seven years ago, my young son, Graham, and his American wife, Dana, returned from the USA. Graham had decided that he did not want to be a professional footballer anymore. He wanted to train to be a nurse. His experience with cancer had incited his interest in nursing. I had heard of a new course in Aberdeen to train as a physician's assistant. This is somewhere between a doctor and a nurse.

Graham secured a place on a two-year course. They were to live on the campus in Aberdeen. Unfortunately for them, but not for me, they had brought with them from the USA, Charlotte, the beautiful, silky grey Great Dane.

She was named after Graham's university town and the place from where she had been abandoned and then rescued by Graham and Dana. As she was not allowed to stay in the apartments in Aberdeen, she came to live with me. She was the most wonderful dog, and we loved her very much. I am now blessed with two beautiful granddaughters.

I was upstairs a few years ago, getting ready to take one of my granddaughters to dancing class, when I tripped and did a full somersault to the bottom of the staircase. Fearing a cracked pelvis, I went for an x-ray.

Fortunately, nothing was broken, but I was in a great amount of pain and could barely walk. For recovery, I required a brain full of oxygen and I needed joy.

I am so lucky to live in the north of Scotland, surrounded by beautiful beaches and mountains. I had a plan to walk on the sand and go into the sea, gradually increasing resistance.

Then I thought about river walking. The River Lossie is tidal, so I would be able to walk with the tide or against the tide and increase my work rate.

Where the river runs in to the sea, there is a beautiful little, old bridge which runs from the road to the beach; at high tide it is the only way to access the beach. I call the bridge my 'Trip Trap Bridge' from the story of *The Billy Goats Gruff.* This was the area where my son Colin was drowned.

Whenever I walk over it, I feel my spirits lift and that Colin's spirit is with me. At low tide, it is possible to cross the river, but it is still waist deep. Each time I go on this walk, the experience is completely different. At low tide it is possible to cross by wading through the river.

Near the rocky edge there are rock pools with teeny, tiny fish which I could feel round my legs. I watch them darting to and fro. I could walk up the river too, against the tide.

Each time I went, there were hundreds of seagulls and just one heron. They used to fly away, startled by me and my giant dog. As time passed, they seemed to get used to me and the heron did not move; he seemed to almost nod, as if he was saying, "Is that you again?"

At high tide I would trip, trap over the rickety bridge and through the beautiful golden sand dunes on to the wide expanse of sparkling beach. I'd splash through the little pools and into the cold but exhilarating North Sea.

Another choice I had at high tide, was to cross the bridge and walk along the riverside through little bunches of pretty, yellow flowers. There were always new things to see, although I did not see anyone else in a bikini, hat and sunglasses!

At the beginning, Charlotte, our dog, did not like the water and would run along the sand when I was in there. Eventually, she learned to walk beside me in the water; her presence adding to the joy in my heart and to the strengthening of my mind and body.

One day, I was feeling very adventurous and decided to walk further up the river. We started off by the sea, went over the sand dunes, and then walked in the river up against the flow. The river began to get more enclosed with hog weed and tall bushes. As the tide came in, the water deepened, too deep to walk, so we got out onto the riverbank.

There was no path and tightly knitted trees and prickly shrubs. Behind these was a twelve-foot bank. My hat and sunglasses vanished in the climb. At the top, we discovered a huge field of cabbages. Taking care not to damage any crops, we walked through the field and finally onto a main road.

The windy country road was narrow, and there was no pavement. Charlotte walked on my inside; I was wearing my bikini and must have looked a sight after scrambling through undergrowth and climbing up a muddy bank.

Several cars tooted as they passed! Eventually, we found a cottage with a man in a garage with a chainsaw and a van.

He said he was working for the owners of the cottage and offered to give me a lift in his van. The van, however, was full of tools and was not suitable for a giant dog. I thanked him and knocked on the cottage door to see if I could borrow a phone and call for some help. I could not get a reply from my husband, nor my sister.

The lovely lady in the house put a blanket around me and drove us back to my car at the Trip Trap bridge. I was very lucky that my adventure ended safely; I didn't try that route again.

It took time, but I strengthened up enough to ski again, and that season I was very happy to be able to do twelve runs.

As you may have gathered, health and wellbeing have been at the top of my life priorities. I made choices to eat fresh and healthy food and have always been able to drink plenty of clear, fresh water every day, with the odd tea and coffee.

I believe that exercise is a must; running, jogging, and walking cost nothing and can easily be incorporated into your life. Any sport is a bonus. After having a hip replacement, I do a lot of river walking, up to my waist, with the fishes, to strengthen my muscles.

I love breathing the energising, salty sea air. Staying healthy requires a coalescence of mind and body; choosing to be happy and having fun and interacting with others helps to maintain a positive mindset and builds resilience.

In the preface to this story, I related the good fortune I had of being introduced to a range of health products by my good friend Kate. Not only have these been revitalising to my memory but also to my overall well-being.

At a dental visit I had an x-ray which showed that I had bad gum disease and bone degeneration. Two years later, my gum disease had disappeared, and the dentist was amazed to see not only a cessation of degeneration but actually regeneration in my bones.

I was also due to have a knee or partial knee replacement and had had two operations to clear pieces of bone and cartilage from my knee. After taking these amazing products, my knee has healed and, in my seventies, I am still going on ski-trips to Canada.

What a kaleidoscope of memories. I can reflect on how lucky I am to be surrounded by loving friends and family and my wonderful husband, who has never clipped my wings, only supported me wholeheartedly.

I am so proud of both of my sons and their achievements as children and now as men. My sister, Hilda, has been my business partner for thirty-eight years, and a constant support through the highs and the lows.

My beautiful grandchildren live across the road from me. There's Kylie age 19, and Raegan age 14. These young ladies have developed into amazing young women. Both are coaching, yes, even Raegan who loves having knowledge to share. They are both involved as founder members of the Abby SPARKLE Foundation, and raise money for children with cancer.

This is our family motto:

BE BRAVE.
BE STRONG.
FEAR NOBODY.
BE KIND.

My colourful life has not always been easy; after Colin's death, I learned to 'not sweat the small stuff'.

I have learnt to not waste time worrying over things you can't change and my favourite quote from John Paul Warren, founder of Voice of the Nations, is 'The cream always rises to the top'.

Above all, I'd like to end by encouraging you to keep on going, keep moving forward, and little by little you will get there.

The End.

Loved the Book?

www.amazon.com

Acknowledgements

Graham Tatters

I have been married to Graham for over forty-six years. He is a man of great integrity, honour and empathy, with an enormous heart, who loves a lot, laughs a lot and gives a lot.

Despite the challenges of my many off-the-wall projects, he has never tried to clip my wings and has supported me throughout everything.

His unwavering love and support have been a continuous and unfailing mainstay, both mentally and physically, through the trials and tribulations of our lives.

He continues to be the most fantastic husband, fantastic father, fantastic grandad, fantastic football manager and fantastic chairman of the Elgin City football team.

Graham is always giving, and he whistles and sings Motown and Soul and continuously spreads joy and happiness. The junior players at the club have a screensaver with him captioned as 'The Legend'.

Rose Turner

A brilliant lady who, after hearing my stories, motivated me to write this book. She pushed and pushed until I started a mind map and then I just continued.

Kylie and Raegan Tatters

Many thanks to my beautiful grandchildren, who helped me to type my first draft. They insisted I got going and kept on going.

Hilda Antley

My thanks go to my wonderful sister, Hilda, for being a wonderful business partner, through every up and every down, who has always loved and supported me and my family.

Author Biography

Paula was born in Ireland, one of six children with entrepreneurial parents who ran two general stores. Although speaking English at home, Paula was sent to a Gaelic speaking school, so these early years were difficult. Adding further difficulty, Paula's parents split up and Paula moved to England, where she then appeared illiterate, unable to read and write in English.

After further moving to and fro between England and Ireland, she settled in school in London to receive a total of two years and nine months of education.

Despite this rocky start, Paula went on to become a PTI in the WRAF, an air hostess and a teacher at a school attended by the royal family. She also set up and ran several successful businesses.

Paula has travelled the world and despite major personal tragedies, has forged an amazing life and been able to bring her dreams to fruition.

Contact the Author

Email:
pmmtatters@gmail.com

Made in the USA
Monee, IL
22 October 2022

16378219R00046